WATER ENERGY

PUTTING WATER TO WORK

JESSIE ALKIRE

Consulting Editor, Diane Craig, M.A./Reading Specialist

Super Sandcastle

An Imprint of Abdo Publishing
abdopublishing.com

abdopublishing.com

Published by Abdo Publishing, a division of ABDO, PO Box 398166, Minneapolis, Minnesota 55439. Copyright © 2019 by Abdo Consulting Group, Inc. International copyrights reserved in all countries. No part of this book may be reproduced in any form without written permission from the publisher. Super SandCastle™ is a trademark and logo of Abdo Publishing.

Printed in the United States of America, North Mankato, Minnesota

052018
092018

THIS BOOK CONTAINS
RECYCLED MATERIALS

Design and Production: Mighty Media, Inc.
Editor: Megan Borgert-Spaniol
Cover Photographs: Shutterstock; Wikimedia Commons
Interior Photographs: Alamy; iStockphoto; Library of Congress; Shutterstock; Wikimedia Commons

Library of Congress Control Number: 2017961859

Publisher's Cataloging-in-Publication Data
Names: Alkire, Jessie, author.
Title: Water energy: Putting water to work / by Jessie Alkire.
Other titles: Putting water to work
Description: Minneapolis, Minnesota : Abdo Publishing, 2019. | Series: Earth's
    energy innovations
Identifiers: ISBN 9781532115752 (lib.bdg.) | ISBN 9781532156472 (ebook)
Subjects: LCSH: Water-power--Juvenile literature. | Power resources--Juvenile
    literature. | Energy development--Juvenile literature. | Energy conversion--
    Juvenile literature.
Classification: DDC 333.914--dc23

Super SandCastle™ books are created by a team of professional educators, reading specialists, and content developers around five essential components—phonemic awareness, phonics, vocabulary, text comprehension, and fluency—to assist young readers as they develop reading skills and strategies and increase their general knowledge. All books are written, reviewed, and leveled for guided reading, early reading intervention, and Accelerated Reader™ programs for use in shared, guided, and independent reading and writing activities to support a balanced approach to literacy instruction.

CONTENTS

WHAT IS WATER ENERGY?

Hydropower dam

Water energy is energy created by moving water. The energy is turned into power. This is called hydropower.

Water energy is a renewable **resource**. Water does not run out. It just changes state. Water energy is also clean. However, hydropower dams can harm wildlife and humans.

Water constantly moves between Earth's surface, oceans, and atmosphere. This is called the water cycle.

ENERGY TIMELINE

200 BCE

People in China use **waterwheels** to power machines.

1870s

Lester Allan Pelton **designs** the Pelton wheel.

1881

Hydropower lights street lamps in Niagara Falls, New York.

Discover how water energy has changed over time!

1882

The first hydropower plant opens in Wisconsin.

1936

The famous Hoover Dam begins operating.

1949

One-third of US electricity comes from hydropower.

WATERWHEELS

Water energy was first used around 200 BCE. People in China used **waterwheels**. Rivers turned the wheels. This created energy that powered machines. Ancient Greeks used waterwheels too.

Water **turbines** were used for mining in the 1800s. Lester Allan Pelton **designed** a new turbine in the 1870s. He called it the Pelton wheel.

Waterwheels were used to grind grain, make paper, and more.

LESTER ALLAN PELTON

BORN: September 5, 1829, Vermilion, Ohio

DIED: March 14, 1908, Oakland, California

Lester Allan Pelton was an American inventor. He moved to California in 1850. Many people had moved there to mine for gold. **Turbines** were used to power the mining machines.

In the 1870s, Pelton created a new kind of turbine. It made better use of water's energy. Pelton's turbine was used in many mines. It was later used to produce electricity!

POWER PLANTS AND DAMS

Water **turbines** produced electricity by the late 1800s. In 1881, hydropower lit streets in Niagara Falls, New York. The first hydropower plant opened in Wisconsin the next year.

Power plants used dams. The Hoover Dam was completed in 1936. By 1949, nearly one-third of US electricity came from hydropower!

Niagara Falls

Hoover Dam is on the border of Nevada and Arizona. It is 726 feet (221 m) tall!

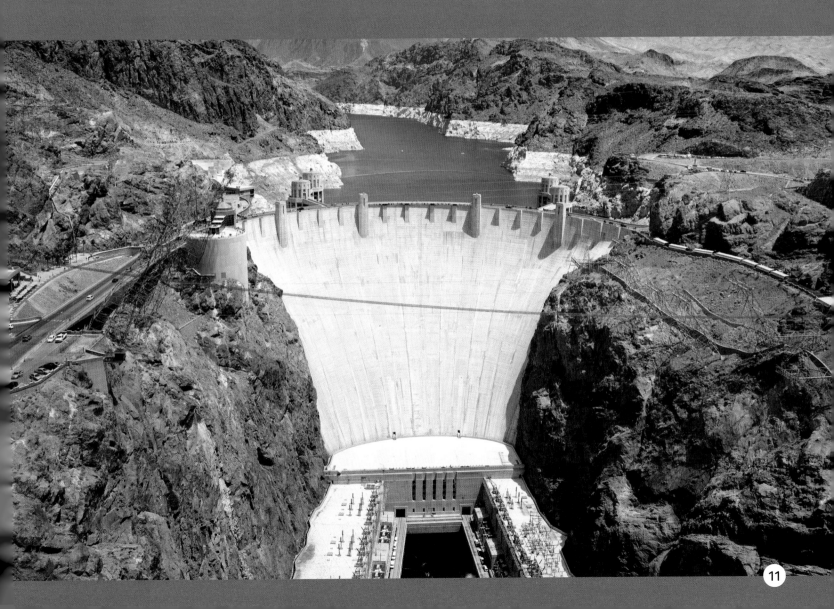

POWERFUL BUT HARMFUL

Today, water is a leading source of renewable energy. Hydropower plants are creating more power than ever!

But hydropower creates some issues. Dams affect river **ecosystems**. They can harm fish populations. Dams can also cause flooding. This affects people who live nearby.

Some dams have fish ladders. These are wide steps that let fish swim around dams.

California's Baldwin Hills Dam broke in 1963. The flood killed five people and destroyed many homes.

MACHINES AND ELECTRICITY

Water energy can still be used to do physical work, such as milling and sawing. But water energy is mainly used to produce electricity.

Hydropower plants are built near large rivers or waterfalls. They take in water as it flows downstream. This captures the energy of flowing water. The energy is turned into electricity.

Sawmill waterwheel

In 2016, hydropower provided about 7 percent of US electricity.

BUILDING POWER

Hydropower dam

Most hydropower plants use dams. Dams stop the flow of water. The water is stored in a **reservoir**. Then the water is **released** when needed.

Some power plants use the natural flow of rivers. Channels direct water into these power plants. Other plants use pumps to store water. Used water is pumped back up into a reservoir. It can be used again when needed!

Grand Coulee Dam is on Washington's Columbia River. It is one of the largest structures ever built by humans!

MAKING ELECTRICITY

Water flows into a power plant. There, it moves through a **turbine**. This makes the turbine spin.

The spinning turbine is connected to a **generator**. The generator turns the turbine's energy into electricity. Power lines send this electricity to homes and businesses!

Hydropower generators

HYDROPOWER PLANT

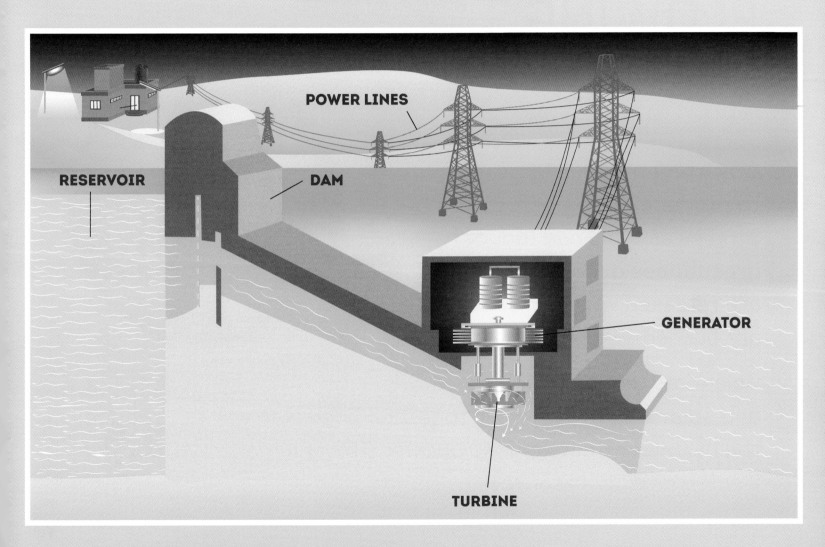

POWER LINES

RESERVOIR

DAM

GENERATOR

TURBINE

FLOWING STRONG

Governments look for ways to produce more hydropower. Studies say this can reduce **greenhouse gases**. These gases are **released** when **fossil fuels** are burned.

Scientists learn how water, wind, and solar energy can work together. They also want to reduce the harmful effects of hydropower. This will make hydropower a safer, cleaner **resource**!

Officials say US hydropower capabilities could grow by 50 percent by 2050.

MORE ABOUT WATER ENERGY

Do you want to tell others about water energy? Here are some fun facts to share!

HYDROPOWER PROVIDES about 16 percent of the world's electricity.

CHINA'S THREE GORGES DAM is the largest hydropower plant in the world.

THE STATE OF WASHINGTON gets more than 70 percent of its electricity from hydropower.

TEST YOUR KNOWLEDGE

1. Is water energy renewable or nonrenewable?

2. When did Lester Allan Pelton **design** the Pelton wheel?

3. Most hydropower is produced by dams. **TRUE OR FALSE?**

THINK ABOUT IT!

Is there a dam near you? Is it used for hydropower?

ANSWERS: 1. Renewable 2. 1870s 3. True

GLOSSARY

design – to plan how something will appear or work.

ecosystem – a group of plants and animals that live together in nature and depend on each other to survive.

fossil fuel – a fuel formed from the remains of plants or animals. Coal, oil, and natural gas are fossil fuels.

generator – a machine that creates electricity.

greenhouse gas – a gas, such as carbon dioxide, that traps heat in Earth's atmosphere.

release – to set free or let go.

reservoir – a natural or human-made place used for storing water.

resource – something that is usable or valuable.

turbine – a machine that produces power when it is rotated at high speed.

waterwheel – a wheel that is turned by water flowing against it.